UNDERSTANDING BREVILLE SMART AIR FRYER OVEN

A Simplified Guide To Quick, Easy, Delicious Affordable, Mouth-Watering Recipes For Weight Loss And Healthier Living

MEREDITH NORA JOHNSON

not engaging in the rendering of legal, financial, medical or professional advice. The content within this book has been derived from various sources. Please consult a licensed professional before attempting any techniques outlined in this book.

By reading this document, the reader agrees that under no circumstances is the author responsible for any losses, direct or indirect, which are incurred as a result of the use of information contained within this document, including, but not limited to, errors, omissions, or inaccuracies.

Table of Contents

INTRODUCTION

The Breville Smart Air Fryer Oven is a conducive way to cook appetizing healthy meals. The machine makes use of fast, hot air to cook the food. This allows the outside of the food to be crisp and also ensures that the inner layers are cooked.

The fryer allows us to cook almost everything and many dishes. We can use the deep fryer for cooking meat, vegetables, poultry, fruits, fish, and a wide variety of desserts.

How does the fryer work?

The innovation of the fryer is very easy and simple. Fried foods have a crisp texture because the hot oil heats the food quickly and equally on its surface. Oil is an excellent conductor of heat, which helps to cook all the ingredients quickly and simultaneously.

For decades, chefs have used transfer ovens to mimic the effects of frying or cooking across the entire surface of the food. But the air never revolves fast enough to achieve this wonderful crunchy surface that we all enjoy in fried foods.

With this process, the air circulates in high degrees, up to 201°C, to "fry" any food such as chicken, fish, or chips, etc. This innovation has changed the whole idea of cooking by reducing fat by up to 80% compared to traditional fried fat.

Cooking the deep fryer releases heat through a heating element that cooks food in a healthier and more convenient way.

There is also an exhaust fan just above the cooking chamber that provides the necessary airflow for the food. In this way, the food is prepared with constant hot air. This leads to the same heating temperature that reaches each part of the food that is cooked. Therefore, only the grill and exhaust fan helps the fryer to propel the air at a constant high speed to cook healthy food with less fat.

Internal pressure increases the temperature, which is then controlled by the exhaust system. The extractor fan also releases additional filtered air to cook food in a much healthier way. The air fryer does not smell at all and is completely harmless, making it easy to use and environmentally friendly.

Benefits of the air fryer:

- Healthier meals without oil
- Eliminate kitchen odors using internal air filters
- Facilitates cleaning due to lack of lubricating oils
- Air Fryers can bake, bake, broil and fry, providing more options.
- Has the ability to adjust and exit from most models and includes a digital timer

The fryer is all-in-one that allows for quick and easy cooking. It also leads to many possibilities once you know it. Once you know the basics and become familiar with your fryer, you can experiment and modify the recipes in any way you prefer. You can prepare a large number of dishes in the fryer and customize your favorite oven to be compatible with the fryer. Everything comes in variety and many options, right?

Cooking perfect, delicious, and healthy meals has never been easier. You can see how this collection of recipes looks.

Enjoy!

1. Scrambled Pancake Hash

Difficulty: Hard

Preparation Time: 5 minutes

Cooking Time: 9 minutes

Servings: 7

Ingredients:

- 1 egg
- ¼ cup heavy cream
- tablespoons butter
- 1 cup coconut flour
- 1 teaspoon ground ginger
- 1 teaspoon salt
- 1 tablespoon apple cider vinegar
- 1 teaspoon baking soda

Directions:

1. Combine the salt, baking soda, ground ginger, and flour in a mixing bowl. In a separate bowl crack, the egg into it.
2. Add butter and heavy cream.
3. Mix well using a hand mixer. Combine the liquid and dry mixtures and stir until smooth.

4. Preheat your air fryer to 400°F. Pour the pancake mixture into the air fryer basket tray.
5. Cook the pancake hash for 4-minutes.
6. After this, scramble the pancake hash well and continue to cook for another 5-minutes.
7. When the dish is cooked, transfer it to serving plates, and serve hot!

Nutrition:

- Calories: 178
- Total Fat: 13.3g
- Carbohydrates: 10.7g
- Protein: 4.4g

2. Onion Frittata

Difficulty: Hard

Preparation Time: 20 minutes

Cooking Time: 30 Minutes

Servings: 6

Ingredients:

- Eggs; whisked
- 1 tablespoon olive oil
- 1 lb. small potatoes; chopped
- 1 oz. cheddar cheese; grated

- ½ cup sour cream
- Yellow onions; chopped
- Salt and black pepper to the taste

Directions:

1. In a large bowl; mix eggs with potatoes, onions, salt, pepper, cheese, and sour cream and whisk well.
2. Grease your air fryer's pan with the oil, add eggs mix; place in the air fryer and cook for 20 minutes at 320 degrees F. Slice frittata, divide among plates and serve for breakfast.

Nutrition:

- Calories: 231
- Fat: 5g
- Fiber: 7g
- Carbohydrates: 8g
- Protein: 4g

3. Pea Tortilla

Difficulty: Very Hard

Preparation Time: 10 minutes

Cooking Time: 17 Minutes

Servings: 8

Ingredients:

- ½ lb. baby peas
- 1 ½ cup yogurt
- Eggs
- ½ cup mint; chopped.
- tablespoon butter
- Salt and black pepper to the taste

Directions:

1. Heat up a pan that fits your air fryer with the butter over medium heat, add peas; mix and cook for a couple of minutes.
2. Meanwhile; in a bowl, mix half of the yogurt with salt, pepper, eggs, and mint and whisk well.
3. Pour this over the peas, toss, introduce in your air fryer and cook at 350°F, for 7 minutes. Spread the rest of the yogurt over your tortilla; slice and serve.

Nutrition:

- Calories: 192
- Fat: 5g
- Fiber: 4g
- Carbohydrates: 8g
- Protein: 7g

4. Mushroom Quiches

Difficulty: Very Hard

Preparation Time: 10 minutes

Cooking Time: 20 Minutes

Servings: 4

Ingredients:

- Button mushrooms; chopped.
- tablespoon ham; chopped
- eggs
- 1 tablespoon flour
- 1 tablespoon butter; soft
- 9-inch pie dough
- ½ teaspoon thyme; dried
- ¼ cup Swiss cheese; grated
- 1 small yellow onion; chopped.
- 1/3 cup heavy cream
- A pinch of nutmeg; ground
- Salt and black pepper to the taste

Directions:

1. Dust a working surface with the flour and roll the pie dough.

2. Press in on the bottom of the pie pan your air fryer has.

3. In a bowl; mix butter with mushrooms, ham, onion, eggs, heavy cream, salt, pepper, thyme, and nutmeg and whisk well.

4. Add this over pie crust, spread, sprinkle Swiss cheese all over and place the pie pan in your air fryer.

5. Cook your quiche at 400°F, for 10 minutes. Slice and serve for breakfast.

Nutrition:

- Calories: 212
- Fat: 4g
- Fiber: 6g
- Carbohydrates: 7g
- Protein: 7g

5. Walnuts Pear Oatmeal

Difficulty: Very Hard

Preparation Time: 10 minutes

Cooking Time: 17 Minutes

Servings: 4

Ingredients:

- 1 tablespoon butter; soft

18

- ¼ cups of brown sugar
- 1 cup water
- ½ cup raisins
- ½ teaspoon cinnamon powder
- 1 cup rolled oats
- ½ cup walnuts; chopped.
- 2 cups pear; peeled and chopped.

Directions:

1. Mix milk with sugar, butter, oats, cinnamon, raisins, pears, and walnuts; stir,
2. Introduce in your fryer and cook at 360°F, for 12 minutes.
3. Divide into bowls and serve.

Nutrition:

- Calories: 230
- Fat: 6g
- Fiber: 11g
- Carbohydrates: 20g
- Protein: 5g

6. Breakfast Raspberry Rolls

Difficulty: Very Hard

Preparation Time: 10 minutes

Cooking Time: 50 minutes

Servings: 6

Ingredients:

- 1 cup milk
- ¼ cup Sugar:
- 1 egg
- tablespoon butter
- ¼ cups flour
- teaspoon yeast

For the filling:

- oz. cream cheese; soft
- oz. raspberries
- 1 teaspoon vanilla extract
- tablespoon Sugar:
- 1 tablespoon cornstarch
- Zest from 1 lemon; grated

Directions:

1. Mix flour with Sugar: and yeast and stir.
2. Add milk and egg, stir until you obtain a dough, leave it aside to rise for 30 minutes; transfer the dough to a working surface, and roll well.
3. Mix cream cheese with sugar, vanilla, and lemon zest; stir well and spread over dough.

4. In another bowl; mix raspberries with cornstarch, stir, and spread over cream cheese mixture.

5. Roll your dough, cut into medium pieces, place them in your air fryer; spray them with cooking spray and cook them at 350°F, for 30 minutes. Serve your rolls for breakfast.

Nutrition:

- Calories: 261
- Fat: 5g
- Fiber: 8g
- Carbohydrates: 9g
- Protein: 6g

7. Bread Pudding

Difficulty: Very Hard

Preparation Time: 10 minutes

Cooking Time: 32 Minutes

Servings: 4

Ingredients:

- ½ lb. white bread; cubed
- 3/4 cup milk
- 3/4 cup water
- 1 teaspoon cinnamon powder

- 1 cup flour
- 3/5 cup brown sugar
- 1 teaspoon cornstarch
- ½ cup apple; peeled; cored and roughly chopped.
- 1 tablespoon honey
- 1 teaspoon vanilla extract
- ½ Soft butter

Directions:

1. In a bowl; mix bread with apple, milk with water, honey, cinnamon, vanilla, and cornstarch, and whisk well.
2. Mix flour with Sugar: and butter and stir until you obtain a crumbled mixture.
3. Press half of the crumble mix on the bottom of your air fryer; add bread and apple mix, add the rest of the crumble and cook everything at 350°F, for 22 minutes. Divide bread pudding on plates and serve.

Nutrition:

- Calories: 261
- Fat: 7g
- Fiber: 7g
- Carbohydrates: 8g
- Protein: 5g

8. Cream Cheese Oats

Difficulty: Very Hard

Preparation Time: 10 minutes

Cooking Time: 35 minutes

Servings: 4

Ingredients:

- 1 cup steel oats
- cups milk
- 1 tablespoon butter
- White Sugar:
- 1 oz. cream cheese; soft
- 3/4 cup raisins
- 1 teaspoon cinnamon powder
- ¼ cup brown Sugar:

Directions:

1. Heat up a pan that fits your air fryer with the butter over medium heat, add oats; stir and toast them for 3 minutes.
2. Add milk and raisins; stir, introduce in your air fryer and cook at 350°F, for 20 minutes.
3. Meanwhile; in a bowl, mix cinnamon with brown Sugar: and stir.

4. In a second bowl; mix white Sugar: with cream cheese and whisk. Divide oats into bowls and top each with cinnamon and cream cheese.

Nutrition:

- Calories: 152
- Fat: 6g
- Fiber: 6g
- Carbohydrates: 25g
- Protein: 7g

9. Bread Rolls

Difficulty: Very Hard

Preparation Time: 10 minutes

Cooking Time: 22 Minutes

Servings: 4

Ingredients:

- Potatoes; boiled; peeled and mashed
- ½ teaspoon turmeric powder
- curry leaf springs
- ½ teaspoon mustard seeds
- Bread slices; white parts only
- 1 coriander bunch; chopped.

- Green chilies; chopped
- Small yellow onions; chopped.
- 2 tablespoon olive oil
- Salt and black pepper to the taste

Directions:

1. Heat up a pan with 1 teaspoon oil; add mustard seeds, onions, curry leaves, and turmeric, stir and cook for a few seconds.
2. Add mashed potatoes, salt, pepper, coriander, and chilies, stir well; take off the heat and cool it down.
3. Divide potatoes mix into 8 parts and shape ovals using your wet hands.
4. Wet bread slices with water; press in order to drain excess water and keep one slice in your palm.
5. Add a potato oval over bread slice and wrap it around it.
6. Do the same with the rest of the potato mix and bread.
7. Heat up your air fryer at 400 degrees F; add the rest of the oil, add bread rolls; cook them for 12 minutes. Divide bread rolls on plates and serve for breakfast.

Nutrition:

- Calories: 261
- Fat: 6g
- Fiber: 9g
- Carbohydrates: 12g
- Protein: 7g

10. Prosciutto Sandwich

Difficulty: Very Easy

Preparation Time: 10 minutes

Cooking Time: 5 minutes

Servings: 1

Ingredients:

- Bread slices
- Mozzarella slices
- Tomato slices
- Prosciutto slices
- Basil leaves
- 1 teaspoon olive oil
- A pinch salt and black pepper

Directions:

1. Arrange mozzarella and prosciutto on a bread slice.
2. Season with salt and pepper, place in your air fryer, and cook at 400 degrees F for 5 minutes.
3. Drizzle oil over prosciutto, add tomato and basil, cover with the other bread slice, cut sandwich in half, and serve.
4. Enjoy!

Nutrition:

- Calories: 172
- Fat 3g
- Fiber: 7g
- Carbs 9g
- Protein: 5g

11. Lentils Fritters

Difficulty: Very Easy

Preparation Time: 10 minutes

Cooking Time: 10 minutes

Servings: 2

Ingredients:

- 1 cup yellow lentils, soaked in water for 1 hour, and drained
- 1 hot chili pepper, chopped
- 1 inch ginger piece, grated
- ½ teaspoon turmeric powder
- 1 teaspoon garam masala
- 1 teaspoon baking powder
- Salt and black pepper to the taste
- teaspoons olive oil

- $1/3$ cup water
- ½ cup cilantro, chopped
- 1 and ½ cup spinach, chopped
- garlic cloves, minced
- ¾ cup red onion, chopped
- Mint chutney for serving

Directions:

1. In your blender, mix lentils with chili pepper, ginger, turmeric, garam masala, baking powder, salt, pepper, olive oil, water, cilantro, spinach, onion, and garlic, blend well and shape medium balls out of this mix.
2. Place them all in your preheated air fryer at 400°F and cook for 10 min. serve your veggie fritters with a side salad for lunch. Enjoy!

Nutrition:

- Calories: 142
- Fat 2g
- Fiber: 8g
- Carbs 12g
- Protein: 4g

12. Lunch Potato Salad

Difficulty: Very Easy

Preparation Time: 10 minutes

Cooking Time: 25 minutes

Servings: 4

Ingredients:

- 1 pound red potatoes, halved
- 2 tablespoons olive oil
- Salt and black pepper to the taste
- 2 green onions, chopped
- 1 red bell pepper, chopped
- 1/3 cup lemon juice
- 2 tablespoons mustard

Directions:

1. On your air fryer's basket, mix potatoes with half of the olive oil, salt, and pepper and cook at 350 degrees F for 25 minutes shaking the fryer once.

2. In a bowl, mix onions with bell pepper and roasted potatoes and toss.

3. In a small bowl, mix lemon juice with the rest of the oil and mustard and whisk really well.

4. Add this to potato salad, toss well and serve for lunch.

5. Enjoy!

Nutrition:

- Calories: 211
- Fat 6g
- Fiber: 8,g
- Carbs 12g
- Protein: 4g

13. Corn Casserole

Difficulty: Easy

Preparation Time: 10 minutes

Cooking Time: 15 minutes

Servings: 4

Ingredients:

- 2 Cups corn
- 2 Tablespoons flour
- 1 egg
- ¼ cup milk
- ½ cup light cream
- 1 ½ cup Swiss cheese, grated
- 1 ½ tablespoons butter
- Salt and black pepper to the taste

- Cooking spray

Directions:

1. In a bowl, mix the corn with flour, egg, milk, light cream, cheese, salt, pepper, and butter and stir well.
2. Grease your air fryer's pan with cooking spray, pour the cream mix, spread, and cook at 320 degrees F for 15 minutes.
3. Serve warm for lunch. Enjoy!

Nutrition:

- Calories: 281
- Fat 7g
- Fiber: 8g
- Carbohydrates: 9g
- Protein: 6g

14. Bacon and Garlic Pizzas

Difficulty: Very Easy

Preparation Time: 10 minutes

Cooking Time: 10 minutes

Servings: 4

Ingredients:

- Dinner rolls, frozen
- Garlic cloves minced

- ½ teaspoon oregano dried
- ½ teaspoon garlic powder
- 1 cup tomato sauce
- Bacon slices, cooked and chopped
- 1 and ¼ cups cheddar cheese, grated
- Cooking spray

Directions:

1. Place dinner rolls on a working surface and press them to obtain 4 ovals.

2. Spray each oval with cooking spray, transfer them to your air fryer and cook them at 370 degrees F for 2 minutes.

3. Spread tomato sauce on each oval, divide garlic, sprinkle oregano and garlic powder, and top with bacon and cheese.

4. Return pizzas to your heated air fryer and cook them at 370 degrees F for 8 minutes more.

5. Serve them warm for lunch. Enjoy!

Nutrition:

- Calories: 217
- Fat 5g
- Fiber: 8g

- Carbohydrates: 12g
- Protein: 4g

15. Sweet and Sour Sausage Mix

Difficulty: Very Easy

Preparation Time: 10 minutes

Cooking Time: 10 minutes

Servings: 4

Ingredients:

- 1 pound sausages, sliced
- 1 red bell pepper, cut into strips
- ½ cup yellow onion, chopped
- Tablespoons brown sugar
- 1/3 cup ketchup
- Tablespoons mustard
- Tablespoons apple cider vinegar
- ½ cup chicken stock

Directions:

1. In a bowl, mix Sugar: with ketchup, mustard, stock, and vinegar and whisk well.

2. In your air fryer's pan, mix sausage slices with bell pepper, onion, and sweet and sour mix, toss and cook at 350 degrees F for 10 minutes.

3. Divide into bowls and serve for lunch.

4. Enjoy!

Nutrition:

- Calories: 162
- Fat 6g
- Fiber: 9g
- Carbohydrates: 12g
- Protein: 6g

16. Ham and Cheese sandwich

Difficulty: Very Hard

Preparation Time: 15 minutes

Cooking time: 20 minutes

Servings: 2

Ingredients:

- 2 Eggs
- 4 Slices of bread of choice
- 2 Slices turkey
- 2 Slices ham
- 1 Tablespoon half and half cream

- 1 Teaspoon melted butter
- 2 Slices Swiss cheese
- ¼ teaspoon pure vanilla extract
- 1 tbsp. powdered sugar: and raspberry jam for serving

Directions:

1. Combine the eggs, vanilla, and cream in a bowl and set aside.
2. Make a sandwich with the bread layered with cheese slice, turkey, ham, cheese slice, and the top slice of bread to make 2 sandwiches. Gently press on the sandwiches to somewhat flatten them.
3. Set your air fryer toast oven to 350 degrees F.
4. Spread out kitchen aluminum foil, cut it about the same size as the sandwich, and spread the melted butter on the foil's surface.
5. Dip the sandwich into the egg mixture and let it soak for about 20 seconds on each side. Repeat this for the other sandwich. Place the soaked sandwiches on the prepared foil sheets, then place them on the basket in your fryer.
6. Cook for 12 minutes, then flip the sandwiches and brush with the remaining butter and cook for another 5 minutes or until well browned.

7. Place the cooked sandwiched on a plate and top with the powdered sugar, and serve with a small raspberry jam bowl.

Nutrition:

- Calories: 735
- Carbohydrates: 13.4g
- Fat: 47.9g
- Protein: 40.8g

17. Classic Fish and Chips

Difficulty: Very Hard

Preparation Time: 15 minutes

Cooking time: 30 minutes

Servings: 4

Ingredients:

- 450g tilapia/ catfish/ cod fillet
- russet potatoes, peeled and cut into French fries (or wedges)
- Vegetable oil
- 1 egg
- 1 cup panko breadcrumbs
- ¼ cup all-purpose flour

- 1 tablespoon sea salt
- Ground pepper to taste

Directions:

1. Toss the prepared potatoes with half the salt, oil, and pepper, if desired.

2. Set your air fryer toast oven to 400 degrees F and cook the potatoes for 15-20 minutes, shaking halfway through to ensure they cook evenly and don't burn.

3. As the potatoes cook, put the flour in a shallow bowl, beat the egg, put in a second bowl, and in a third bowl the panko crumbs.

4. Dredge the fillet pieces, one a time, in the flour, egg, and panko.

5. Cook the fish for 15 minutes at 330 degrees F, flipping halfway through cook time.

6. Serve hot with your favorite sauces. Enjoy!

Nutrition:

- Calories: 307
- Carbohydrates: 31.2g
- Fat: 9.1g
- Protein: 25.8g

18. Seasoned Catfish

Difficulty: Hard

Preparation Time: 15 minutes

Cooking Time: 23 minutes

Servings: 4

Ingredients:

- (4-oz.) catfish fillets
- Italian seasoning
- Salt and ground black pepper, as required
- 1 tablespoon olive oil
- 1 tablespoon fresh parsley, chopped

Directions:

1. Rub the fish fillets with seasoning, salt, and black pepper generously, and then coat with oil.
2. Push the Temp button and rotate the dial to set the temperature at 400 degrees F.
3. When the unit beeps to show that it is preheated, open the lid.
4. Arrange the fish fillets in a greased "Air Fry Basket" and insert it in the oven.
5. Flip the fish fillets once halfway through.

6. Serve hot with the garnishing of parsley.

Nutrition:

- Calories: 205
- Total Fat 14.2g
- Saturated Fat: 2.4g
- Cholesterol: 58mg
- Sodium: 102mg
- Total Carbohydrates: 0.8g
- Fiber: 0g
- Sugar: 0.6g
- Protein: 17.7g

19. Crispy Catfish

Difficulty: Hard

Preparation Time: 15 minutes

Cooking Time: 15 minutes

Servings: 5

Ingredients:

- (6-oz.) catfish fillets
- 1 cup milk
- Teaspoons fresh lemon juice
- ½ cup yellow mustard

- ½ cup cornmeal
- ¼ cup all-purpose flour
- Tablespoons dried parsley flakes
- ¼ teaspoon red chili powder
- ¼ teaspoon cayenne pepper
- ¼ teaspoon onion powder
- ¼ teaspoon garlic powder
- Salt and ground black pepper, as required
- Olive oil cooking spray

Directions:

1. In a large bowl, place the catfish, milk, and lemon juice and refrigerate for about 15 minutes.
2. In a shallow bowl, add the mustard.
3. In another bowl, mix the cornmeal, flour, parsley flakes, and spices.
4. Remove the catfish fillets from the milk mixture, and with paper towels, pat them dry.
5. Coat each fish fillet with mustard and then roll into cornmeal mixture.
6. Then, spray each fillet with the cooking spray.
7. When the unit beeps to show that it is preheated, open the lid.
8. Assemble the catfish fillets in an "Air Fry Basket" in the oven

9. After 10 minutes of cooking, flip the fillets and spray with the cooking spray.

10. Serve hot.

Nutrition:

- Calories: 340
- Total Fat 15.5g
- Saturated Fat: 3.1g
- Cholesterol: 84mg
- Sodium: 435mg
- Total Carbohydrates: 18.3g
- Fiber: 2g
- Sugar: 2.7g
- Protein: 30.9g

20. Cornmeal Coated Catfish

Difficulty: Hard

Preparation Time: 15 minutes

Cooking Time: 14 minutes

Servings: 4

Ingredients:

- Cornmeal
- Teaspoons Cajun seasoning

- ½ teaspoon paprika
- ½ teaspoon garlic powder
- Salt, as required
- (6-oz.) catfish fillets
- 1 tablespoon olive oil

Directions:

1. In a bowl, mix the cornmeal, Cajun seasoning, paprika, garlic powder, and salt.
2. Add the catfish fillets and coat with the mixture. Now, coat each fillet with oil.
3. When the unit beeps to show that it is preheated, open the lid.
4. Arrange the catfish fillets in a greased "Air Fry Basket" and insert them in the oven.
5. After 10 minutes of cooking, flip the fillets and spray with the cooking spray. Serve hot

Nutrition:

- Calories: 161
- Total Fat 10.1g
- Saturated Fat: 1.7g
- Cholesterol: 40mg
- Sodium: 110mg
- Total Carbohydrates: 3.3g
- Fiber: 0.4g

- Sugar: 0.1g
- Protein: 13.7g

21. Breaded Flounder

Difficulty: Hard

Preparation Time: 15 minutes

Cooking Time: 12 minutes

Servings: 3

Ingredients:

- 1 egg
- 1 cup dry breadcrumbs
- ¼ cup vegetable oil
- (6-oz.) flounder fillets
- 1 lemon, sliced

Directions:

1. Beat the egg in a bowl.
2. Put in the breadcrumbs and oil in a bowl and mix until a crumbly mixture is formed.
3. Dip flounder fillets into the beaten egg and then coat with the breadcrumb mixture.
4. When the unit beeps to show that it is preheated, open the lid.

5. Arrange the flounder fillets in a greased "Air Fry Basket" and insert it in the oven.
6. Set off with the lemon slices and serve hot.

Nutrition:

- Calories: 524
- Total Fat 24.2g
- Saturated Fat: 5.1g
- Cholesterol: 170mg
- Sodium: 463mg
- Total Carbohydrates: 26.5g
- Fiber: 1.5g
- Sugar: 2.5g
- Protein: 47.8g

22. Carrot & Zucchini Muffins

Difficulty: Very Hard

Preparation Time: 5 minutes

Cooking Time: 14 minutes

Servings: 4

Ingredients:

- Butter, melted
- ¼ cup carrots, shredded
- ½ cup zucchini, shredded
- 1 ½ cups almond flour
- 1 tablespoon liquid Stevia
- teaspoons baking powder
- A pinch salt
- eggs
- 1 tablespoon yogurt
- 1 cup milk

Directions:

1. Preheat your air fryer to 350°F.
2. Beat the eggs, yogurt, milk, salt, pepper, baking soda, and Stevia.
3. Whisk in the flour gradually.

4. Add zucchini and carrots.

5. Grease muffin tins with butter and pour the muffin batter into containers. Cook for 14-minutes and serve.

Nutrition:

- Calories: 224
- Total Fats: 12.3g
- Carbohydrates: 11.2g
- Protein: 14.2g

23. Curried Cauliflower Florets

Difficulty: Very Hard

Preparation Time: 5 minutes

Cooking Time: 10 minutes

Servings: 4

Ingredients:

- ¼ cup sultanas or golden raisins
- ¼ teaspoon salt
- 1 tablespoon curry powder
- 1 head cauliflower, broken into small florets
- ¼ cup pine nuts
- ½ cup olive oil

Directions:

1. In a cup of boiling water, soak your sultanas to plump. Preheat your air fryer to 350°F.
2. Add oil and pine nuts to the air fryer and toast for a minute or so.
3. In a bowl toss the cauliflower and curry powder as well as salt, then add the mix to the air fryer mixing well.
4. Cook for 10-minutes. Drain the sultanas, toss with cauliflower, and serve.

Nutrition:

- Calories: 275
- Total Fat: 11.3g
- Carbohydrates: 8.6g
- Protein: 9.5g

24. Crispy Rye Bread Snacks with Guacamole and Anchovies

Difficulty: Very Hard

Preparation Time: 10 minutes

Cooking Time: 10 minutes

Servings: 4

Ingredients:

- 8 Slices of rye bread
- 1 Guacamole
- 8 Anchovies in oil

Directions:

1. Cut each slice of bread into 3 strips of bread.
2. Place in the basket of the air fryer, without piling up, and we go in batches giving it the touch you want to give it. You can select 350°F, 10 minutes.
3. When you have all the crusty rye bread strips, put a layer of guacamole on top, whether homemade or commercial.
4. In each bread, place 2 anchovies on the guacamole.

Nutrition:

- Calories: 180
- Fat: 11.6g
- Carbohydrates: 16g
- Protein: 6.2g
- Sugar: 0g
- Cholesterol: 19.6mg

25. Oat and Chia Porridge

Difficulty: Very Hard

Preparation Time: 5 minutes

Cooking Time: 5 minutes

Servings: 4

Ingredients:

- 4 tablespoons peanut butter
- 2 teaspoons liquid Stevia
- 1 tablespoon butter, melted
- 2 cups milk
- 2 cups oats
- 1 cup chia seeds

Directions:

1. Preheat your air fryer to 390°F.
2. Whisk the peanut butter, butter, milk and Stevia in a bowl.
3. Stir in the oats and chia seeds.
4. Pour the mixture into an oven-proof bowl and place in the air fryer and cook for 5-minutes.

Nutrition:

- Calories: 228
- Total Fats: 11.4g
- Carbohydrates: 10.2g
- Protein: 14.5g

26. Feta & Mushroom Frittata

Difficulty: Very Hard

Preparation Time: 15 minutes

Cooking Time: 30 minutes

Servings: 4

Ingredients:

- 1 red onion, thinly sliced
- 2 cups button mushrooms, thinly sliced
- Salt to taste
- 3 tablespoons feta cheese, crumbled
- 4 medium eggs
- Non-stick cooking spray
- 2 tablespoons olive oil

Directions:

1. Sauté the onion and mushrooms in olive oil over medium heat until the vegetables are tender.
2. Remove the vegetables from the pan and drain on a paper towel-lined plate.
3. In a mixing bowl, whisk eggs and salt. Coat all sides of the baking dish with cooking spray.
4. Preheat your air fryer to 325 degrees Fahrenheit. Pour the beaten eggs into the prepared baking dish and scatter the sautéed vegetables and crumble feta

on top. Bake in the air fryer for 30-minutes. Allow to cool slightly and serve!

Nutrition:

- Calories: 226
- Total Fat: 9.3g
- Carbohydrates: 8.7g
- Protein: 12.6g

27. Butter Glazed Carrots

Difficulty: Very Hard

Preparation Time: 20 Minutes

Cooking Time: 15 minutes

Servings: 4

Ingredients:

- 2 cups of baby carrots
- 1 tablespoon brown Sugar:
- ½ tablespoon butter; melted
- A pinch salt and black pepper

Directions:

1. Take a baking dish suitable to fit in your air fryer. Toss carrots with sugar, butter, salt, and black peppers in that baking dish.

2. Place this dish in the air fryer basket and seal the fryer. Cook the carrots for 10 minutes at 3500 F on Air fryer mode. Enjoy.

Nutrition:

- Calories: 151
- Fat: 2g
- Fiber: 4g
- Carbs 14g
- Protein: 4g

28. Risotto Bites

Difficulty: Medium

Preparation Time: 15 minutes

Cooking Time: 10 minutes

Servings: 4

Ingredients:

- 1½ cups cooked risotto
- Tablespoons Parmesan cheese, grated
- ½ egg, beaten
- 1½ oz. mozzarella cheese, cubed
- 1/3 cup breadcrumbs

Directions:

1. In a bowl, add the risotto, Parmesan, and egg and mix until well combined.
2. Make 20 equal-sized balls from the mixture.
3. Insert a mozzarella cube in the center of each ball.
4. With your fingers, smooth the risotto mixture to cover the ball.
5. In a shallow dish, place the breadcrumbs.
6. Coat the balls with the breadcrumbs evenly.

7. Press the "Power Button" of the Air Fryer Oven and turn the dial to select the "Air Fry" mode.
8. Press the Time button and again turn the dial to set the cooking time to 10 minutes.
9. Now push the Temp button and rotate the dial to set the temperature at 390 degrees F.
10. Press the "Start/Pause" button to start.
11. When the unit beeps to show that it is preheated, open the lid.
12. Arrange the balls in "Air Fry Basket" and insert them in the oven.
13. Serve warm.

Nutrition:

- Calories: 340
- Total Fat 4.3g
- Saturated Fat: 2g
- Cholesterol: 29mg
- Sodium: 173mg
- Total Carbohydrates: 62.4g
- Fiber: 1.3g
- Sugar: 0.7g
- Protein: 11.3g

29. Rice Flour Bites

Difficulty: Medium

Preparation Time: 15 minutes

Cooking Time: 12 minutes

Servings: 4

Ingredients:

- Milk
- ½ teaspoon vegetable oil
- ¾ cup rice flour
- 1 oz. Parmesan cheese, shredded

Directions:

1. In a bowl, add milk, flour, oil, and cheese and mix until a smooth dough forms.
2. Make small equal-sized balls from the dough.
3. Press the "Power Button" of the Air Fryer Oven and turn the dial to select the "Air Fry" mode.
4. Press the Time button and again turn the dial to set the cooking time to 12 minutes.
5. Now push the Temp button and rotate the dial to set the temperature at 300 degrees F.
6. Press the "Start/Pause" button to start.
7. When the unit beeps to show that it is preheated, open the lid.

8. Arrange the balls in "Air Fry Basket" and insert them in the oven.
9. Serve warm.

Nutrition:

- Calories: 148
- Total Fat: 3g
- Saturated Fat: 1.5g
- Cholesterol: 7mg
- Sodium: 77mg
- Total Carbohydrates: 25.1g
- Fiber: 0.7g
- Sugar: 1.1g
- Protein: 4.8g

30. Lemon Parmesan and Peas Risotto

Difficulty: Hard

Preparation Time: 10 minutes

Cooking Time: 17 minutes

Servings: 6

Ingredients:

- 1 tablespoons butter
- 1½ cup rice

- 1 yellow onion, peeled and chopped
- 1 tablespoon extra-virgin olive oil
- 1 teaspoon lemon zest, grated
- 3½ cups chicken stock
- tablespoons lemon juice
- Parsley, diced
- Parmesan cheese, finely grated
- Salt and ground black pepper, to taste
- 1½ cup peas

Directions:

1. Put the Instant Pot in the sauté mode, add 1 tablespoon butter and oil, and heat them. Add the onion, mix, and cook for 5 minutes.
2. Add the rice, mix, and cook for another 3 minutes.
3. Add 3 cups of broth and lemon juice, mix, cover, and cook for 5 minutes on rice.
4. Release the pressure, put the fryer in manual mode, add the peas and the rest of the broth, stir and cook for 2 minutes.
5. Add the cheese, parsley, remaining butter, lemon zest, salt, and pepper to taste and mix.
6. Divide between plates and serve.

Nutrition:

- Calories: 140
- Fat: 1.5
- Fiber: 1
- Carbohydrate: 27
- Proteins: 5

31. Spinach and Goat Cheese Risotto

Difficulty: Hard

Preparation Time: 10 minutes

Cooking Time: 10 minutes

Servings: 6

Ingredients:

- ¾ cup yellow onion, chopped
- 1½ cups Arborio rice
- 4 ounces spinach, chopped
- 3½ cups hot vegetable stock
- ½ cup white wine
- 2 garlic cloves, peeled and minced
- 2 tablespoons extra virgin olive oil
- Salt and ground black pepper, to taste
- 1/3 cup pecans, toasted and chopped

- 3 ounces goat cheese, soft and crumbled
- 2 tablespoons lemon juice

Directions:

1. Put the Instant Pot in the sauté mode, add the oil and heat. Add garlic and onion, mix and cook for 5 minutes. Add the rice, mix, and cook for 1 minute. Add wine, stir and cook until it is absorbed.

2. Add 3 cups of stock, cover the Instant Pot, and cook the rice for 4 minutes.

3. Release the pressure, uncover the Instant Pot, add the spinach, stir and cook for 3 minutes in Manual mode. Add salt, pepper, the rest of the stock, lemon juice, and goat cheese, and mix. Divide between plates, decorate with nuts and serve.

Nutrition:

- Calories: 340
- Fat: 23
- Fiber: 4.5
- Carbohydrate: 24
- Proteins: 18.9

32. Rice and Artichokes

Difficulty: Hard

Preparation Time: 10 minutes

Cooking Time: 20 minutes

Servings: 4

Ingredients:

- 2 Garlic cloves, peeled and crushed
- 1¼ cups chicken broth
- 1 tablespoon extra-virgin olive oil
- 4 ounces Arborio rice
- 1 tablespoon white wine
- 4 ounces canned artichoke hearts, chopped
- 3 ounces cream cheese
- 1 tablespoon grated Parmesan cheese
- 1½ tablespoons fresh thyme, chopped
- Salt and ground black pepper, to taste
- 3 ounces graham cracker crumbs
- 1¼ cups water

Directions:

1. Put the Instant Pot in the sauté mode, add the oil, heat, add the rice, and cook for 2 minutes.

2. Add the garlic, mix, and cook for 1 minute.

3. Transfer to a heat-resistant plate.

4. Add the stock, crumbs, salt, pepper, wine, mix, and cover the dish with aluminum foil.

5. Place the dish in the basket to cook the Instant Pot, add water, cover, and cook for 8 minutes on rice.

6. Release the pressure, remove the plate, uncover, and add cream cheese, parmesan, artichoke hearts, and thyme. Mix well and serve.

Nutrition:

- Calories: 240
- Fat: 7.2
- Fiber: 5.1
- Carbohydrate: 34
- Proteins: 6

33. Potatoes Au Gratin

Difficulty: Hard

Preparation Time: 10 minutes

Cooking Time: 17 minutes

Servings: 6

Ingredients:

- ½ cup yellow onion, chopped

- 1 tablespoons butter
- 1 cup chicken stock
- 6 potatoes, peeled and sliced
- ½ cup sour cream
- Salt and ground black pepper, to taste
- 1 cup Monterey jack cheese, shredded
- For the topping:
- 2 tablespoons melted butter
- 1 cup breadcrumbs

Directions:

1. Put the Instant Pot in Sauté mode, add the butter, and melt. Add the onion, mix and cook for 5 minutes. Add the stock, salt, and pepper, and put the steamer basket in the Instant Pot also.

2. Add the potatoes, cover the Instant Pot and cook for 5 minutes in the Manual setting. In a bowl, mix 3 tablespoons of butter with breadcrumbs and mix well. Relieve the pressure of the Instant Pot, remove the steam basket and transfer the potatoes to a pan.

3. Pour the cream and cheese into the instant pot and mix. Add the potatoes and mix gently.

4. Spread breadcrumbs, mix everywhere, place on a preheated grill, and cook for 7 minutes. Let cool for more minutes and serve.

Nutrition:

- Calories: 340
- Fat: 22g
- Fiber: 2g
- Carbohydrate: 32g
- Proteins: 11g

34. Cinnamon Banana Bread

Difficulty: Easy

Preparation Time: 15 minutes

Cooking Time: 20 minutes

Servings: 8

Ingredients:

- 1 ^{1}/3 cups flour

- 2/3 cup Sugar:

- 1 teaspoon baking soda

- 1 teaspoon baking powder

- 1 teaspoon ground cinnamon

- 1 teaspoon salt

- ½ cup milk

- ½ cup olive oil

- bananas, peeled and sliced

Directions:

1. In the bowl of a stand mixer, add all the ingredients and mix well. Grease a loaf pan.

2. Place the mixture into the prepared pan. Press "Power Button" of Air Fryer Oven and turn the dial to select the "Air Crisp" mode. Press the Time button and again turn the dial to set the time to 20 minutes

3. Now push the Temp button and rotate the dial to set the temperature at 330 degrees F.

4. Press the "Start/Pause" button to start. When the unit beeps to show that it is preheated, open the lid.

5. Arrange the pan in "Air Fry Basket" and insert it in the oven. Place the pan onto a wire rack to cool for about 10 minutes. Carefully, invert the bread onto a wire rack to cool completely before slicing.

6. Cut the bread into desired-sized slices and serve.

Nutrition:

- Calories: 295
- Fat 13.3g
- Carbs 44g
- Protein: 3.1g

35. Banana & Walnut Bread

Difficulty: Easy

Preparation Time: 15 minutes

Cooking Time: 25 minutes

Servings: 10

Ingredients:

- 1½ cups self-rising flour
- ¼ teaspoon bicarbonate of soda
- tablespoons plus 1 teaspoon butter
- 2/3 cup plus ½ tablespoon caster sugar
- medium eggs
- 3½ oz. walnuts, chopped
- cups bananas, peeled and mashed

Directions:

1. In a bowl, mix the flour and bicarbonate of soda.
2. In another bowl, add the butter, and Sugar: and beat until pale and fluffy.
3. Add the eggs, one at a time along with a little flour, and mix well.
4. Stir in the remaining flour and walnuts.
5. Add the bananas and mix until well combined.
6. Grease a loaf pan. Place the mixture into the prepared pan.
7. Press "Power Button" of Air Fryer Oven and turn the dial to select the "Air Crisp" mode.
8. Press the Time button and again turn the dial to set the cooking time to 10 minutes

9. Now push the Temp button and rotate the dial to set the temperature at 355 degrees F.

10. Press the "Start/Pause" button to start.

11. When the unit beeps to show that it is preheated, open the lid.

12. Arrange the pan in "Air Fry Basket" and insert it in the oven.

13. After 10 minutes of cooking, set the temperature at 338 degrees F for 15 minutes

14. Place the pan onto a wire rack to cool for about 10 minutes

15. Carefully, invert the bread onto a wire rack to cool completely before slicing.

16. Cut the bread into desired-sized slices and serve.

Nutrition:

- Calories: 270
- Fat 12.8g
- Carbs 35.5g
- Protein: 5.8g

36. Banana & Raisin Bread

Difficulty: Easy

Preparation Time: 15 minutes

Cooking Time: 40 minutes

Servings: 6

Ingredients:

- 1½ cups cake flour
- 1 teaspoon baking soda
- ½ teaspoon ground cinnamon
- Salt, to taste
- ½ cup vegetable oil
- Eggs
- ½ cup sugar
- ½ teaspoon vanilla extract
- medium bananas, peeled and mashed
- ½ cup raisins, chopped finely

Directions:

1. In a large bowl, mix the flour, baking soda, cinnamon, and salt.

2. In another bowl, beat well eggs and oil.

3. Add the sugar, vanilla extract, and bananas and beat until well combined.

4. Add the flour mixture and stir until just combined.

5. Place the mixture into a lightly greased baking pan and sprinkle with raisins.

6. With a piece of foil, cover the pan loosely.

7. Press the "Power Button" of Air Fryer Oven and turn the dial to select the "Air Bake" mode.

8. Press the Time button and again turn the dial to set the cooking time to 30 minutes

9. Now push the Temp button and rotate the dial to set the temperature at 300 degrees F.

10. Press the "Start/Pause" button to start.

11. When the unit beeps to show that it is preheated, open the lid.

12. Arrange the pan in "Air Fry Basket" and insert it in the oven.

13. After 30 minutes of cooking, set the temperature to 285 degrees F for 10 minutes

14. Place the pan onto a wire rack to cool for about 10 minutes

15. Carefully, invert the bread onto a wire rack to cool completely before slicing.

16. Cut the bread into desired-sized slices and serve.

Nutrition:

- Calories: 448
- Fat 20.2g
- Carbs 63.9g
- Protein: 6.1g

37. 3-Ingredients Banana Bread

Difficulty: Medium

Preparation Time: 10 minutes

Cooking Time: 20 minutes

Servings: 6

Ingredients:

- (6.4-oz.) banana muffin mix
- 1 cup water
- 1 ripe banana, peeled and mashed

Directions:

1. In a bowl, add all the ingredients and with a whisk, mix until well combined.
2. Place the mixture into a lightly greased loaf pan.

3. Press the "Power Button" of Air Fryer Oven and turn the dial to select the "Air Bake" mode.

4. Press the Time button and again turn the dial to set the cooking time to 20 minutes

5. Now push the Temp button and rotate the dial to set the temperature at 360 degrees F.

6. Press the "Start/Pause" button to start.

7. When the unit beeps to show that it is preheated, open the lid.

8. Arrange the pan in "Air Fry Basket" and insert it in the oven.

9. Place the pan onto a wire rack to cool for about 10 minutes

10. Carefully, invert the bread onto a wire rack to cool completely before slicing. Cut the bread into desired-sized slices and serve.

Nutrition:

- Calories: 144
- Fat 3.8g
- Carbs 25.5g
- Protein: 1.9 g

38. Yogurt Banana Bread

Difficulty: Medium

Preparation Time: 15 minutes

Cooking Time: 28 minutes

Servings: 5

Ingredients:

- 1 medium very ripe banana, peeled and mashed
- 1 large egg
- 1 tablespoon canola oil
- 1 tablespoon plain Greek yogurt
- ¼ teaspoon pure vanilla extract
- ½ cup all-purpose flour
- ¼ cup granulated white Sugar:
- ¼ teaspoon ground cinnamon
- ¼ teaspoon baking soda
- ⅛ teaspoon sea salt

Directions:

1. In a bowl, add the mashed banana, egg, oil, yogurt, vanilla, and beat until well combined.

2. Add the flour, sugar, baking soda, cinnamon, and salt and mix until just combined.

3. Place the mixture into a lightly greased mini loaf pan.

4. Press the "Power Button" of Air Fryer Oven and turn the dial to select the "Air Bake" mode.

5. Press the Time button and again turn the dial to set the cooking time to 28 minutes

6. Now push the Temp button and rotate the dial to set the temperature at 350 degrees F.

7. Press the "Start/Pause" button to start. When the unit beeps to show that it is preheated, open the lid.

8. Arrange the pan in "Air Fry Basket" and insert it in the oven.

9. Place the pan onto a wire rack to cool for about 10 minutes

10. Carefully, invert the bread onto a wire rack to cool completely before slicing.

11. Cut the bread into desired-sized slices and serve.

Nutrition:

- Calories: 145
- Fat 4g
- Carbs 25g
- Protein: 3g

39. Sour Cream Banana Bread

Difficulty: Medium

Preparation Time: 15 minutes

Cooking Time: 37 minutes

Servings: 8

Ingredients:

- ¾ cup all-purpose flour
- ¼ teaspoon baking soda
- ¼ teaspoon salt
- Ripe bananas, peeled and mashed
- ½ cup Granulated sugar
- ¼ cup sour cream
- ¼ cup vegetable oil
- 1 large egg
- ½ teaspoon pure vanilla extract

Directions:

1. In a large bowl, mix the flour, baking soda, and salt.

2. In another bowl, add the bananas, egg, sugar, sour cream, oil, and vanilla and beat until well combined.

3. Add the flour mixture and mix until just combined.

4. Place the mixture into a lightly greased pan. Press "Power Button" of Air Fryer Oven and turn the dial to select the "Air Crisp" mode.

5. Press the Time button and again turn the dial to set the cooking time to 37 minutes

6. Now push the Temp button and rotate the dial to set the temperature at 310 degrees F. Press the "Start/Pause" button to start.

7. When the unit beeps to show that it is preheated, open the lid. Arrange the pan in "Air Fry Basket" and insert it in the oven.

8. Place the pan onto a wire rack to cool for about 10 minutes

9. Carefully, invert the bread onto a wire rack to cool completely before slicing.

10. Cut the bread into desired-sized slices and serve.

Nutrition:

- Calories: 201
- Fat 9.2g
- Carbs 28.6g
- Protein: 2.6g

40. Peanut Butter Banana Bread

Difficulty: Medium

Preparation Time: 15 minutes

Cooking Time: 40 minutes

Servings: 6

Ingredients:

- 1 cup + 1 tablespoon all-purpose flour

- ¼ teaspoon baking soda

- 1 teaspoon baking powder

- ¼ teaspoon salt

- 1 large egg

- 1/3 cup Granulated sugar

- ¼ cup canola oil

- tablespoons creamy peanut butter

- tablespoons sour cream

- 1 teaspoon vanilla extract

- medium ripe bananas, peeled and mashed

- ¾ cup walnuts, roughly chopped

Directions:

1. In a bowl and mix the flour, baking powder, baking soda, and salt.
2. In another large bowl, add the egg, sugar, oil, peanut butter, sour cream, and vanilla extract and beat until well combined.
3. Add the bananas and beat until well combined.
4. Add the flour mixture and mix until just combined.
5. Gently, fold in the walnuts.
6. Place the mixture into a lightly greased pan.
7. Press "Power Button" of Air Fryer Oven and turn the dial to select the "Air Crisp" mode.
8. Press the Time button and again turn the dial to set the cooking time to 40 minutes
9. Now push the Temp button and rotate the dial to set the temperature at 330 degrees F.
10. Press the "Start/Pause" button to start.
11. When the unit beeps to show that it is preheated, open the lid.
12. Arrange the pan in "Air Fry Basket" and insert it in the oven.
13. Place the pan onto a wire rack to cool for about 10 minutes
14. Carefully, invert the bread onto a wire rack to cool completely before slicing.

15. Cut the bread into desired-sized slices and serve.

Nutrition:

- Calories: 384
- Fat 23g
- Carbs 39.3g
- Protein: 8.9g

DESSERTS

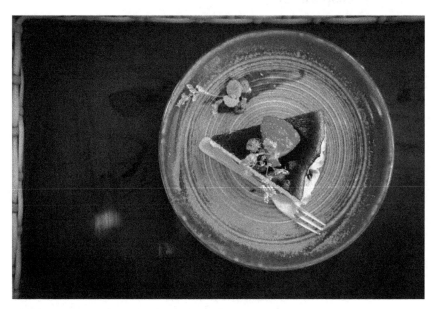

41. Lobster tails with lemon butter

Difficulty: Hard

Preparation Time: 10 minutes

Cooking Time: 8 minutes

Servings: 4

Ingredients:

- Lobster tails, shell cut from the top
- 1 tablespoon fresh parsley, chopped
- garlic cloves, pressed
- 1 teaspoon Dijon mustard
- ¼ teaspoon salt
- ⅛ teaspoon black pepper
- 1 ½ tablespoon olive oil
- 1 ½ tablespoon fresh lemon juice
- 1 tablespoon butter, divided

Directions:

1. Place the lobster tails in the oven's baking tray.
2. Whisk the rest of the ingredients in a bowl and pour over the lobster tails.
3. Press the "power button" of the Air Fryer Oven and turn the dial to select the "broil" mode.
4. Press the time button and again turn the dial to set the cooking time to 8 minutes.

5. Now push the temp button and rotate the dial to set the temperature at 350 degrees f.
6. Once preheated, place the lobster's baking tray in the oven and close its lid.
7. Serve warm.

Nutrition:

- Calories: 281
- Total fat: 18.1g
- Saturated Fat: 8.4g
- Cholesterol: 242mg
- Sodium: 950mg
- Total Carbohydrates: 0.8g
- Dietary Fiber: 0.1g
- Total sugars: 0.2g
- Protein: 27.9g

42. Sheet pan seafood bake

Difficulty: Hard

Preparation Time: 10 minutes

Cooking Time: 14 minutes

Servings: 4

Ingredients:

- Corn ears, husked and diced
- 1 lb. (453.592g) red potatoes, boiled, diced
- lbs. (907.185g) Clams, scrubbed
- 1 lb. (453.592g) Shrimp, peeled and de-veined
- Sausage, sliced
- ½ red onion, sliced
- Lobster tails, peeled
- Black pepper to taste
- 1 lemon, cut into wedges
- 1 cup butter
- Minced garlic
- 1 tablespoon old bay seasoning
- Fresh parsley for garnish

Directions:

1. Toss all the veggies, corn, seafood, oil, and seasoning in a baking tray.
2. Press the "power button" of the Air Fryer Oven and turn the dial to select the "broil" mode.
3. Press the time button and again turn the dial to set the cooking time to 14 minutes.
4. Now push the temp button and rotate the dial to set the temperature at 425 degrees f.
5. Once preheated, place the seafood's baking tray in the oven and close its lid.

6. Serve warm.

Nutrition:

- Calories: 532
- Total fat 35.6g
- Saturated Fat: 18.8g
- Cholesterol: 219mg
- Sodium: 1379mg
- Total Carbohydrates: 26.3g
- Dietary Fiber: 2.5g
- Total sugars 4.4
- Protein: 28.7g

43. Orange sponge cake

Difficulty: Hard

Preparation Time: 50 minutes

Cooking Time: 14 minutes

Servings: 6

Ingredients:

- 2 oz. sugar
- 8 oz. self-rising flour
- 3 oz. butter
- 2 eggs

- 1 teaspoon baking powder
- 1 teaspoon vanilla extract
- Zest 1 orange

Frosting:

- 3 egg whites
- Juice of 1 orange
- 1 teaspoon orange food coloring
- Zest of 1 orange
- 3 oz. superfine sugar

Directions:

1. Preheat Breville on bake function to 160°F and place all cake ingredients, in a bowl, and beat with an electric mixer. Transfer half of the batter into a prepared cake pan; bake for 15 minutes. Repeat the process for the other half of the batter.
2. Meanwhile, prepare the frosting by beating all frosting ingredients together. Spread the frosting mixture on top of one cake. Top with the other cake.

Nutrition:

- Calories: 828
- Protein: 11.46g
- Fat: 39.77g
- Carbohydrates: 107.89g

44. Apricot crumble with blackberries

Difficulty: Hard

Preparation Time: 30 minutes

Cooking Time: 14 minutes

Servings: 4

Ingredients:

- ½ cups fresh apricots, de-stoned and cubed
- 1 cup fresh blackberries
- ½ cup sugar
- tablespoon lemon juice
- 1 cup flour
- Salt as needed
- tablespoon butter

Directions:

1. Add the apricot cubes to a bowl and mix with lemon juice, 2 tablespoon sugar, and blackberries. Scoop the mixture into a greased dish and spread it evenly. In another bowl, mix flour and remaining sugar.

2. Add 1 tablespoon of cold water and butter and keep mixing until you have a crumbly mixture. Preheat Breville on bake function to 390°F and place the fruit

mixture in the basket. Top with crumb mixture and cook for 20 minutes.

Nutrition:

- Calories: 546
- Protein: 7g
- Fat: 5.23g
- Carbohydrates: 102.53g

45. Apple & cinnamon pie

Difficulty: Hard

Preparation Time: 30 minutes

Cooking Time: 14 minutes

Servings: 9

Ingredients:

- 4 Apples, diced
- 3 oz. butter, melted
- 4 oz. sugar
- 1 oz. brown sugar
- 1 teaspoon cinnamon
- 1 egg, beaten
- 1 Large puff pastry sheets
- ¼ teaspoon salt

Directions:

1. Whisk white sugar, brown sugar, cinnamon, salt, and butter, together. Place the apples in a baking dish and coat them with the mixture. Place the baking dish in the toaster oven, and cook for 10 minutes at 350°F on bake function.

2. Meanwhile, roll out the pastry on a floured flat surface, and cut each sheet into 6 equal pieces. Divide the apple filling between the components. Brush the edges of the pastry squares with the egg.

3. Fold them and seal the edges with a fork. Place on a lined baking sheet and cook in the fryer at 350°F for 8 minutes. Flip over, increase the temperature to 390°F, and cook for 2 more minutes.

Nutrition:

- Calories: 140
- Protein: 1.28g
- Fat: 6.33g
- Carbohydrates: 21.19g

46. Spicy Shrimp Kebab

Difficulty: Medium

Preparation Time: 25 minutes

Cooking Time: 20 minutes

Servings: 4

Ingredients:

- 1 ½ pounds jumbo shrimp, cleaned, shelled, and deveined
- 1-pound cherry tomatoes
- tablespoons butter, melted
- 1 tablespoons sriracha sauce
- Sea salt and ground black pepper
- ½ teaspoon dried oregano
- ½ teaspoon dried basil
- 1 teaspoon dried parsley flakes
- ½ teaspoon marjoram
- ½ teaspoon mustard seeds

Directions:

1. Toss all elements in a mixing bowl until the shrimp and tomatoes are covered on all sides.

2. Let the wooden skewers be soaked in water for 15 minutes.

3. Thread the jumbo shrimp and cherry tomatoes onto skewers. Cook in the preheated air fryer at a temperature of 400 degrees f for 5 minutes, working with batches.

Nutrition:

- Calories: 247
- Fat 8.4g
- Carbohydrates: 6g
- Protein: 36.4g
- Sugars: 3.5g
- Fiber: 8g

47. Crumbed Fish Fillets with Tarragon

Difficulty: Medium

Preparation Time: 25 minutes

Cooking Time: 20 minutes

Servings: 4

Ingredients:

- Eggs, beaten
- ½ teaspoon tarragon
- Fish fillets, halved
- 2 tablespoons dry white wine

- 1-3 cup parmesan cheese, grated
- 1 teaspoon seasoned salt
- 1-3 teaspoon mixed peppercorns
- ½ teaspoon fennel seed

Directions:

1. Add the parmesan cheese, salt, peppercorns, fennel seeds, and tarragon to your food processor; blitz for about 20 seconds.

2. Drizzle fish fillets with dry white wine. Dump the egg into a shallow dish.

3. Now, coat the fish fillets with the beaten egg on all sides; then, coat them with the seasoned cracker mix.

4. Air-fry at 345 degrees f for about 17 minutes.

Nutrition:

- Calories: 305
- Fat: 17.7g
- Carbohydrates: 6.3g
- Protein: 27.2g
- Sugars: 0.3g
- Fiber: 0.1g

48. Smoked and Creamed White Fish

Difficulty: Medium

Preparation Time: 20 minutes

Cooking Time: 15 minutes

Servings: 4

Ingredients:

- ½ tablespoon yogurt
- 1/3 cup spring garlic, finely chopped
- Fresh chopped chives, for garnish
- eggs, beaten
- ½ teaspoon dried dill weed
- 1 teaspoon dried rosemary
- 1/3 cup scallions, chopped
- 3 cup smoked white fish, chopped
- 1/½ tablespoons crème Fraiche
- 1 teaspoon kosher salt
- 1 teaspoon dried marjoram
- 1/3 teaspoon ground black pepper, or more to taste
- Cooking spray

Directions:

1. Firstly, spritz four oven-safe ramekins with cooking spray. Then, divide smoked whitefish, spring garlic, and scallions among greased ramekins.

2. Crack an egg into each ramekin; add the crème, yogurt, and all seasonings.

3. Now, air-fry approximately 13 minutes at 355 degrees f. Taste for doneness and eat warm garnished with fresh chives.

Nutrition:

- Calories: 249
- Fat: 22.1g
- Carbohydrates: 7.6g
- Protein: 5.3g
- Sugars: 3.1g
- Fiber: 0.7g

49. Parmesan and Paprika Baked Tilapia

Difficulty: Medium

Preparation Time: 20 minutes

Cooking Time: 15 minutes

Servings: 6

Ingredients:

- 1 cup parmesan cheese, grated
- 1 teaspoon paprika
- 1 teaspoon dried dill weed

- pounds tilapia fillets
- $1/3$ cup mayonnaise
- ½ tablespoon lime juice
- Salt and ground black pepper, to taste

Directions:

1. Mix the mayonnaise, parmesan, paprika, salt, black pepper, and dill weed until everything is thoroughly combined.

2. Then, drizzle tilapia fillets with lime juice.

3. Cover each fish fillet with parmesan mayo mixture; roll them in parmesan paprika mixture. Bake to your fryer at 335 for about 10 minutes. Serve and eat warm.

Nutrition:

- Calories: 294
- Fat: 16.1g
- Carbohydrates: 2.7g
- Protein: 35.9g
- Sugars: 0.1g
- Fiber: 0.2g

50. Tangy Cod Fillets

Difficulty: Medium

Preparation Time: 20 minutes

Cooking Time: 15 minutes

Servings: 2

Ingredients:

- 1 ½ tablespoons sesame oil

- ½ heaping teaspoon dried parsley flakes

- 1/3 teaspoon fresh lemon zest, finely grated

- medium-sized cod fillets

- 1 teaspoon sea salt flakes

- A pinch of salt and pepper

- 1/3 teaspoon ground black pepper, or more to savor

- ½ tablespoon fresh lemon juice

Directions:

1. Set the air fryer to cook at 375 degrees f. Season each cod fillet with sea salt flakes, black pepper, and dried parsley flakes. Now, drizzle them with sesame oil.

2. Place the seasoned cod fillets in a single layer at the bottom of the cooking basket; air-fry for approximately 10 minutes. While the fillets are cooking, prepare the sauce by mixing the other

ingredients. Serve cod fillets on four individual plates garnished with the creamy citrus sauce.

Nutrition:

- Calories: 291
- Fat: 11.1g
- Carbohydrates: 2.7g
- Protein: 41.6g
- Sugars: 1.2g
- Fiber: 0.5g

51. Fish and Cauliflower Cakes

Difficulty: Medium

Preparation Time: 2 hours 20 minutes

Cooking Time: 13 minutes

Servings: 4

Ingredients:

- ½-pound cauliflower florets
- ½ teaspoon English mustard
- tablespoons butter, room temperature
- ½ tablespoon cilantro, minced

- tablespoons sour cream

- ½ cups cooked white fish

- Salt and freshly cracked black pepper, to savor

Directions:

1 Boil the cauliflower until tender. Then, purée the cauliflower in your blender. Transfer to a mixing dish.

2 Now, stir in the fish, cilantro, salt, and black pepper.

3 Add the sour cream, English mustard, and butter; mix until everything's well incorporated. Using your hands, shape into patties.

4 Place inside the refrigerator for around 2 hours. Cook in your fryer for 13 minutes at 395 degrees F. Serve with some extra English mustard.

Nutrition:

- Calories: 285
- Fat: 15.1g
- Carbohydrates: 4.3g
- Protein: 31.1g
- Sugars: 1.6g
- Fiber: 1.3g

52. Chicken Nuggets

Difficulty: Medium

Preparation Time: 10 Minutes

Cooking Time: 20 Minutes

Servings: 4

Ingredients:

- 1 pound boneless, skinless chicken breasts
- Chicken seasoning or rub
- Salt
- Pepper
- Eggs
- 1 tablespoon bread crumbs
- 1 tablespoon panko bread crumbs
- Cooking oil

Directions:

1. Preparation of ingredients. Cut the chicken breasts into 1-inch pieces.

2. In a large bowl, add together the chicken pieces with the chicken seasoning, salt, and pepper.

3. In a small bowl, beat the eggs. In another bowl, combine breadcrumbs and countertop.

4. Dip the chicken pieces in the eggs and then the breadcrumbs.

5. Place the pepitas in the deep fryer. Don't overdo the basket. Cook in batches. Drizzle the seeds with cooking oil.

6. Air Frying. Cook for 4 minutes. Open the air fryer oven and shake the basket. Set temperature to 360°F. Cook for an additional 4 minutes. Remove the cooked nuggets from the Air fryer oven, repeat steps 5 and 6 for the remaining chicken nuggets. Cool before serving.

Nutrition:

- Calories: 206
- Fat: 5g
- Protein: 31g
- Fiber: 1g

53. Cheesy Chicken Fritters

Difficulty: Medium

Preparation Time: 5 Minutes

Cooking Time: 20 Minutes

Servings: 17

Ingredients:

Chicken Fritters:

- ½ teaspoon salt
- ⅛ teaspoon pepper
- 1 ½ tablespoon fresh dill
- 1 ¹/3 cup shredded mozzarella cheese
- ¹/3 cup coconut flour
- ¹/3 cup vegan mayo
- Eggs
- 1 ½ pounds chicken breasts

Garlic Dip:

- ⅛ teaspoon pepper
- ¼ teaspoon salt
- ½ tablespoon lemon juice
- 1 pressed garlic cloves
- ¹/3 cup vegan mayo

Directions:

1. Preparing the Ingredients. Slice chicken breasts into ¹/3" pieces and place in a bowl. Add all remaining fritter ingredients to the bowl and stir well. Cover and chill for 2 hours or overnight.

2. Ensure your air fryer is preheated to 350 degrees. Spray basket with a bit of olive oil.

3. Air Frying. Add marinated chicken to the Air fryer oven. Set temperature to 350°F, set time to 20 minutes, and cook 20 minutes, making sure to turn halfway through the cooking process.

4. To make the dipping sauce, combine all the dip ingredients until smooth.

Nutrition:

- Calories: 467
- Fat: 27g
- Protein: 21g
- Sugar: 3g

54. Air Fryer Chicken Parmesan

Difficulty: Medium

Preparation Time: 5 Minutes

Cooking Time: 9 Minutes

Servings: 4

Ingredients:

- ½ cup keto marinara
- 1 tablespoon mozzarella cheese
- 1 tablespoon melted ghee

- 1 tablespoon grated parmesan cheese

- 1 tablespoon gluten-free seasoned breadcrumbs

- 8-ounce chicken breasts

Directions:

1. Preparing the Ingredients. Ensure the air fryer is preheated to 360 degrees. Spray the basket with olive oil.

2. Mix parmesan cheese and breadcrumbs together. Melt ghee.

3. Brush melted ghee onto the chicken and dip into breadcrumb mixture.

4. Place coated chicken in the air fryer and top with olive oil.

5. Air Frying. Set temperature to 360°F, and set time to 6 minutes. Cook 2 breasts for 6 minutes and top each breast with a tablespoon sauce and 1½ tablespoons of mozzarella cheese. Cook another 3 minutes to melt the cheese.

6. Keep cooked pieces warm as you repeat the process with the remaining breasts.

Nutrition:

- Calories: 251

- Fat: 10g
- Protein: 31g
- Sugar: 0g

55. Ricotta and Parsley Stuffed Turkey Breasts

Difficulty: Medium

Preparation Time: 5 Minutes

Cooking Time: 25 Minutes

Servings: 4

Ingredients:

- 1 turkey breast, quartered
- 1 cup Ricotta cheese
- ¼ cup fresh Italian parsley, chopped
- 1 teaspoon garlic powder
- ½ teaspoon cumin powder
- 1 egg, beaten
- 1 teaspoon paprika
- Salt and ground black pepper, to taste
- Crushed tortilla chips
- 1 ½ tablespoons extra-virgin olive oil

Directions:

1. Preparing the Ingredients. Firstly, flatten out each piece of turkey breast with a rolling pin. Prepare three mixing bowls.

2. In a shallow bowl, combine Ricotta cheese with parsley, garlic powder, and cumin powder.

3. Place the Ricotta/parsley mixture in the middle of each piece. Repeat with the remaining pieces of the turkey breast and roll them up.

4. In another shallow bowl, whisk the egg together with paprika. In the third shallow bowl, combine the salt, pepper, and crushed tortilla chips.

5. Dip each roll in the whisked egg, then, roll them over the tortilla chips mixture.

6. Transfer prepared rolls to the Oven rack/basket. Drizzle olive oil over all. Place the tray Rack on the middle-shelf of the Air fryer oven. Air Frying. Cook for 25 minutes at 350 degrees F, working in batches. Serve warm, garnished with some extra parsley, if desired.

Nutrition:

- Calories: 509
- Fat: 23g
- Protein: 26g
- Fiber: 5g

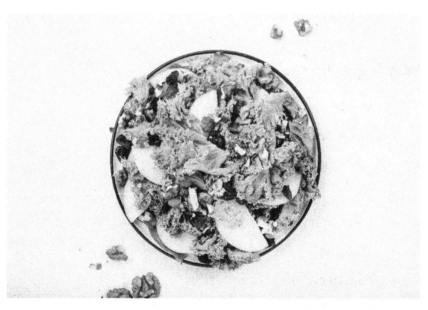

56. Vegan Pear and Cranberry Cake

Difficulty: Medium

Preparation Time: 5 minutes

Cooking Time: 45 minutes

Servings: 4-6

Ingredients:

Dry Ingredients:

- 1 ¼ cup whole wheat pastry flour
- ⅛ teaspoon sea salt
- ½ teaspoon baking powder
- ½ teaspoon baking soda
- ½ teaspoon ground cardamom

Wet Ingredients:

- ½ cup unsweetened nondairy milk
- tablespoons coconut oil
- tablespoons ground flax seeds
- ¼ cup agave
- 1 ½ cups water
- Mix-Ins
- ½ cup chopped cranberries
- 1 cup chopped pear

Directions:

1. Grease a Bundt pan; set aside.
2. In a mixing, mix all dry ingredients together.
3. In another bowl, mix all wet ingredients; whisk the wet ingredients into the dry until smooth. Fold in the add-ins and spread the mixture into the pan; cover with foil. Place pan in your air fryer toast oven and add water in the bottom and bake at 370 degrees F for 35 minutes.
4. When done, use a toothpick to check for doneness. If it comes out clean, then the cake is ready, if not, bake for 5-10 more minutes, checking frequently to avoid burning.
5. Remove the cake and let stand for 10 minutes before transferring from the pan. Enjoy!

Nutrition:

- Calories: 309
- Carbohydrates: 14.7g
- Fat: 27g
- Protein: 22.6g

57. Air fryer toast oven Steamed Broccoli

Difficulty: Very Easy

Preparation Time: 8 minutes

Cooking Time: 3 minutes

Servings: 2

Ingredients:

- 1 pound broccoli florets
- 1½ cups water
- Salt and pepper to taste
- I teaspoon extra virgin olive oil

Directions:

1 Add water to the bottom of your air fryer toast oven and set the basket on top.
2 Toss the broccoli florets with, salt pepper, and olive oil until evenly combined then transfer to the basket of your air fryer toast oven.
3 Cook at 350 degrees for 5 minutes.
4 Remove the basket and serve the broccoli.

Nutrition:

- Calories: 160
- Carbohydrates: 6.1g
- Fat: 12g
- Protein: 13g